Magnets

Pulling Together, Pushing Apart

Written by Natalie M. Rosinsky
Illustrated by Sheree Boyd

Content Advisor: Dr. Paul Ohmann, Assistant Professor of Physics, University of St. Thomas, St. Paul, Minnesota
Reading Advisor: Lauren A. Liang, M.A., Literacy Education, University of Minnesota, Minneapolis, Minnesota

AMAZING SCIENCE

PICTURE WINDOW BOOKS
Minneapolis, Minnesota

Editor: Nadia Higgins
Designer: Melissa Voda
Page production: The Design Lab
The illustrations in this book were prepared digitally.

PICTURE WINDOW BOOKS
1710 Roe Crest Drive
North Mankato, MN 56003
www.capstonepub.com

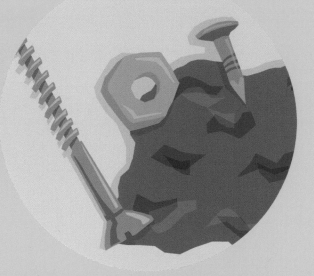

Library of Congress Cataloging-in-Publication Data
Rosinsky, Natalie M. (Natalie Myra)
  Magnets : pulling together, pushing apart / written by
Natalie M. Rosinsky ; illustrated by Sheree Boyd.
    p. cm. — (Amazing science) Includes bibliographical
references and index.
  ISBN 978-1-4048-0014-4 (library binding)
  ISBN 978-1-4048-0333-6 (softcover)
  1. Magnets—Juvenile literature. 2. Magnetism—Juvenile
literature. [1. Magnets. 2. Magnetism.] I. Boyd, Sheree,
ill. II. Title.
  QC753.7 .R68 2003
  538—dc21   2002005779

Printed in the United States   5664

TABLE OF CONTENTS

Amazing Magnets

Magnets have the amazing power to make things move. When strings pull and lift things, it's easy to see how they work. Magnets seem to make things move by magic.

Watch a paper clip
scoot to a magnet.
The paper clip slides
along as if pulled by
an invisible string.

Magnets pull only on special kinds of metal.
Try to move a steel spoon or an iron nail
with a magnet. Now try a ball of cotton, a
rubber ball, or a plastic pen.

How Do Magnets Work?

Magnets can only pull on things that are close enough to them.

Put a paper clip far away from a magnet. Slowly move the paper clip closer and closer. How close does it get before it leaps toward the magnet?

Magnets can work through a covering, if it is thin enough. Lay a sheet of paper over your magnet and place the paper clip on top of the paper. Or try putting a piece of plastic wrap or the corner of your shirt on top of the magnet. What happens to the paper clip now?

Dangle an iron nail from the end of a magnet. Now touch a paper clip to the nail. The paper clip sticks to the nail.

The nail has become a magnet. When some metal objects touch or get close enough to magnets, the metal objects become magnets.

8

Pull the nail away from the magnet. Does the paper clip still cling to the nail?

Rub a steel spoon along a magnet. You can feel the spoon being pulled toward the magnet's ends. These ends are called poles.

A magnet's power is strongest at its two ends. One end is called the north pole. The other is the south pole.

Fun fact: If you break a magnet apart, you have two new magnets. Each separate piece has its own north and south poles.

The poles of a magnet can push as well as pull.

Poles that are alike repel each other. The north pole of one magnet will push away from the north pole of another.

Fun fact: In Japan, some high-speed trains use extra strong magnets. Magnets on the train repel, or push against, magnets in the track. The train seems to glide on a cushion of air.

Opposite poles attract each other. One magnet's north pole will stick to the south pole of another magnet.

13

Magnetic Earth

Earth is a giant magnet.
It has two ends, or poles,
just like other magnets.
Earth's magnetic ends are
close to the North and
South Poles that are shown
on a globe or map.

S

N

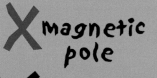

X magnetic
pole

South

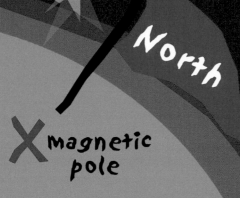

North

X magnetic pole

The cold North Pole and South Pole, covered with ice, are not the same as Earth's two magnetic poles.

How Does a Compass Work?

Earth's magnetic power pulls other magnets. The needle on a compass is a tiny magnet. The needle always lines up in a north-south direction, pointing toward the magnetic poles of Earth.

Fun fact: A compass won't work if you are standing too close to the cold North Pole. The needle points to Earth's magnetic pole. Once you travel past that magnetic pole, the needle does not point northward anymore.

A compass shows us what direction we are moving in—north, south, east, or west. Sailors once used compasses to cross the ocean and find their way back home.

Magnets All Around

Some of Earth's rocks have magnetic powers. Long ago, the Greek and Chinese people discovered the rock magnetite.

Fun fact: Another name for a piece of magnetite is a lodestone. Lodestones were used to make the world's first compasses.

The Greeks were amazed as they watched magnetite pull small pieces of iron. The ancient Chinese hung splinters of magnetite from strings and watched the rocks line up in a north-south direction.

Today, electric fans whirl, refrigerators hum, and burglar alarms ring with the help of magnets in their motors.

Huge magnets help junkyard workers lift tons of scrap metal. These magnets move cars and trucks as if they were small toys. Doctors also use magnets in special machines to look deep inside your body.

Magnets push and pull us all around the world.

Experiments

Find a Magnet's Poles: With an adult's help, crumble a steel wool pad into small bits. (Make sure to put on gloves if you use your hands to break up the wool pad.) Sprinkle these bits all around a small bar magnet. What parts of the magnet do they rush to? These parts are the poles, the strongest parts of a magnet. Do the experiment again. Do you see the same pattern?

Make Your Own Compass: Tie a string around the middle of a small bar magnet. Lift the string and let the magnet dangle. See how it spins around to point in one direction? One end points toward the North Pole of Earth, the other points south. Carry the string and magnet around the room. The magnet will keep pointing in the same direction.

Turn an Iron Nail into a Magnet: Rub an iron nail along a magnet 20 times. Rub in the same direction every time. Your iron nail is now a magnet. Take the nail around the room. What things stick to it?

Make a Magnet with Electricity: Some magnets are made by electricity. These magnets are useful because they can be turned on and off. People use them to make electric motors that power all kinds of things around your house, like fans, hair dryers, can openers, and vacuum cleaners.

You can make your own magnet with electricity. Here's an activity to do with your class or your family.

WHAT YOU WILL NEED:

An adult to help you

A battery (AA, C, or D size)

A piece of metal wire about 1 foot (30 centimeters) long

An iron nail

Tape

Wrap the wire 10 times around the nail. Tape one end of the wire to the side of the battery with the plus sign (+). Tape the other end to the side with the minus sign (-). Your iron nail is now an electromagnet. It works just like a regular magnet.

What happens to the nail when you remove the wire from the battery? Is it still a magnet?

Plan a Hidden Treasure Hunt: You can use compasses for a great family or classroom adventure. Ask some adults to make up a hidden treasure hunt. Here's how it works: They hide treasures around a park, a school, or your house. Then they give you directions to each one, like "Walk 100 steps east. Then take 25 steps south." Use your compass to figure out the directions you should move in. Remember, since a compass always points north, you can easily discover the other directions.

Glossary

attract—to pull something toward something else

compass—a tool that uses a magnet to help people find their way. A compass needle points north.

electromagnet—a magnet that is made with electricity

magnetite—a magnetic rock

poles—the two strongest places on a magnet. Opposite poles attract each other. Alike poles repel each other.

repel—to push something away

To Learn More

At the Library

Branley, Franklyn Mansfield. What Makes a Magnet? New York: HarperCollins, 1996.

Stille, Darlene R. Magnets. Minneapolis: Compass Point Books, 2001.

Woodruff, John. Magnetism. Austin, Tex.: Raintree Steck-Vaughn, 1998.

On the Web

FactHound offers a safe, fun way to find Web sites related to topics in this book. All of the sites on FactHound have been researched by our staff.

1. Go to www.facthound.com

2. Type in this special code: 140480014X

3. Click the FETCH IT button.

Your trusty FactHound will fetch the best sites for you!

Index